STUDIES IN ECONOMIC

This series, specially commissioned by the Economic History Society, provides a guide to the current interpretations of the key themes of economic and social history in which advances have recently been made or in which there has been significant debate.

Originally entitled 'Studies in Economic History', in 1974 the series had its scope extended to include topics in social history, and the new series title, 'Studies in Economic and Social History', signalises this development.

The series gives readers access to the best work done, helps them to draw their own conclusions in major fields of study, and by means of the critical bibliography in each book guides them in the selection of further reading. The aim is to provide a springboard to further work rather than a set of pre-packaged conclusions or short-cuts.

ECONOMIC HISTORY SOCIETY

The Economic History Society, which numbers over 3000 members, publishes the *Economic History Review* four times a year (free to members) and holds an annual conference. Enquiries about membership should be addressed to the Assistant Secretary, Economic History Society, Peterhouse, Cambridge. Full-time students may join the Society at special rates.

STUDIES IN ECONOMIC AND SOCIAL HISTORY

Edited for the Economic History Society by M. W. Flinn

PUBLISHED

OTHER TITLES ARE IN PREPARATION

British Trade Unions
1875–1933

Prepared for
the Economic History Society by

JOHN LOVELL

Senior Lecturer in Economic and Social History,
University of Kent

First published 1977 by
THE MACMILLAN PRESS LTD
London and Basingstoke
Associated companies in New York Dublin
Melbourne Johannesburg and Madras

SBN 333 17926 9

Printed in Great Britain by
THE ANCHOR PRESS LTD
Tiptree, Essex

Contents

Note on References

References in the text within square brackets refer to the numbered items of the Bibliography, followed where appropriate, by the page number in italics, e.g. [68 : *350*] or by the chapter or part number in roman, e.g. [50 : *ch.* 8].

Caption to Cover Illustration

The Woes of Unity House
[Dedicated to the Officials at Unity House and their pathetic efforts to check this modern tendency on the part of the Rank and File to outgrow Institutions.]

Trades Union Officials (to the Boy-Who-Would-Grow-Up) :
'Here, I say, think of us. This Growth has got to stop !'

Editor's Preface

SO long as the study of economic and social history was confined to a small group at a few universities, its literature was not prolific and its few specialists had no great problem in keeping abreast of the work of their colleagues. Even in the 1930s there were only two journals devoted exclusively to economic history and none at all to social history. But the high quality of the work of the economic historians during the inter-war period and the post-war growth in the study of the social sciences sparked off an immense expansion in the study of economic history after the Second World War. There was a great expansion of research and many new journals were launched, some specialising in branches of the subject like transport, business or agricultural history. Most significantly, economic history began to be studied as an aspect of history in its own right in schools. As a consequence, the examining boards began to offer papers in economic history at all levels, while textbooks specifically designed for the school market began to be published. As a specialised discipline, social history is an even more recent arrival in the academic curriculum. Like economic history, it, too, is rapidly generating a range of specialist publications. The importance of much of the recent work in this field and its close relationship with economic history have therefore prompted the Economic History Society to extend the scope of this series – formerly confined to economic history – to embrace themes in social history.

For those engaged in research and writing this period of rapid expansion of studies has been an exciting, if rather breathless one. For the larger numbers, however, labouring in the outfield of the schools and colleges of further education, the excitement of the explosion of research has been tempered by frustration arising from its vast quantity and, frequently, its controversial character. Nor, it must be admitted, has the ability or willingness of the academic historians to generalise and summarise marched in step with their enthusiasm for research.

The greatest problems of interpretation and generalisation have tended to gather round a handful of principal themes in economic and social history. It is, indeed, a tribute to the sound sense of economic and social historians that they have continued to dedicate their energies, however inconclusively, to the solution of these key problems. The results of this activity, however, much of it stored away in a wide range of academic journals, have tended to remain inaccessible to many of those currently interested in the subject. Recognising the need for guidance through the burgeoning and confusing literature that has grown around these basic topics, the Economic History Society hopes in this series of short books to offer some help to students and teachers. The books are intended to serve as guides to current interpretations in major fields of economic and social history in which important advances have recently been made, or in which there has recently been some significant debate. Each book aims to survey recent work, to indicate the full scope of the particular problem as it has been opened up by recent scholarship, and to draw such conclusions as seem warranted, given the present state of knowledge and understanding. The authors will often be at pains to point out where, in their view, because of a lack of information or inadequate research, they believe it is premature to attempt to draw firm conclusions. While authors will not hesitate to review recent and older work critically, the books are not intended to serve as vehicles for their own specialist views: the aim is to provide a balanced summary rather than an exposition of the author's own viewpoint. Each book will include a descriptive bibliography.

In this way the series aims to give all those interested in economic and social history at a serious level access to recent scholarship in some major fields. Above all, the aim is to help the reader to draw his own conclusions, and to guide him in the selection of further reading as a means to this end, rather than to present him with a set of pre-packaged conclusions.

M. W. FLINN

University of Edinburgh   *Editor*

1 False Dawn – Trade Unionism after 1875

THE early 1870s can be represented as something of a false dawn for trade unionism in the United Kingdom. The legal battles were fought and apparently won in 1871 and 1875, and during the economic boom of the period total trade union membership expanded at a rapid rate.

The expansion was of qualitative as well as quantitative significance. New unions were established outside the traditional spheres of influence – organisations of gas-stokers, dockers, agricultural labourers and other lower-paid workers. Even white-collar workers were affected: the National Union of Elementary Teachers was set up in 1870. In a well-known article, G. D. H. Cole drew attention to the magnitude of these developments and to what he believed to be their implications for labour history.

> In the boom of the early 1870s [he wrote] the Trade Union movement was on the point of assuming the character which it took on more definitely in the 1880s, with the foundation of the Miners' Federation, the revolt of the dock workers and the match-girls, and the creation of a host of new unions among less skilled manual workers and also in non-manual occupations. But for the Great Depression which began in the middle seventies, British Labour would not have waited until 1889 before asserting itself as a movement of the whole labour class against exploitation [23].

For Cole, then, the onset of the Great Depression after 1873 cut short an expansion that was in the process of converting British trade unionism into a class-conscious mass movement; not until the later 1880s was progress again resumed.

Cole's emphasis on new growth and activity in the early

9

seventies was important, and much more recently A. E. Musson has also stressed the new horizons that were opening up for unionism in this period [50 : *ch.* 8]. But it is implied in Cole's interpretation that the period between 1875 and 1888 was moribund; and this view may be questioned. It is a traditional view. The Webbs certainly regarded the period as barren. It is true that they noted the success with which many unions withstood the economic onslaught of the later 1870s, and concluded that the 'trials of 1879 proved that the Trade Union Movement was at last beyond all danger of destruction or collapse, and that the Trade Union organisation had become a permanent element in our social structure' [68 :*350*]. Beyond this, however, they thought little of the performance of the unions during these years, and devoted scant space to industrial developments. Their main concern was with the political shortcomings of the trade union leaders, an issue which has also preoccupied certain modern writers on the period [1 : *ch.* 12].

One crucial point to be borne in mind in any reappraisal of the post-1875 period is that trade union experience varied between one industry or occupation and another. The Webbs themselves noted what they called an 'increasing differentiation of policy and interest' amongst the unions [68 :*350*], but this simply led them into a discussion of the problems of sectionalism and demarcation disputes. H. A. Clegg, in a paper criticising their treatment of this period, suggested that it is necessary to begin by drawing a broad distinction between the experience of the craft unions and that of the rest of the movement [18 :*9*].

The craft unions, he argued, were not hit really hard by the wage reductions of the late seventies, and in any case had made good their losses by 1883. Regarding membership, he noted: 'Having maintained their membership between 1874 and 1879, the six major craft unions rose from a total of 108,000 in 1879 to 134,000 in 1883.' Clegg argued further that the notion that the craft societies were moribund and ineffective stemmed from a misunderstanding of their method of functioning. They combined a centralised financial administration with a decentralised trade policy. National leaders might make pronouncements about moderation and conciliation, but it was the local men who

10

handled trade matters. At local level the union sometimes bargained directly with employers at *ad hoc* conferences over alterations to wages and hours. Local collective bargaining of this kind was certainly increasing in the craft trades during the 1870s and 1880s and was usually encouraged by union leaders. Such bargaining activity was, however, intermittent, and in its absence union branches sought to impose their rules unilaterally. Where an employer refused to pay the local union rate, or otherwise flouted its rules, the union's elaborate friendly benefits were there to enable men to remain in idleness rather than work under non-union conditions. Such a method of operation meant that the union was in the main able to operate effectively without major confrontations with the employers. Viewed at the national level therefore craft societies appeared pacific, stagnant bodies, devoid of an active trade policy. The Webbs were content to leave the reader with such a picture, even though they were well aware of the system of unilateral regulation, which they called the Method of Mutual Insurance [69 : *Pt* 2], upon which craft societies relied at local level.

It seems reasonable to suggest, then, that so far as the major craft unions were concerned the period 1875–88 was one of steady expansion and continuing effectiveness. The same holds true for the cotton unions, although their method of operation was very different from that of the crafts. But what of the others? The expansion of the non-craft organisations had been a major feature of the early seventies, and it was the growth in this sector which most attracted the attention of Cole and other historians. With the onset of depression these unions mostly suffered a steep decline in membership, and many passed out of existence. The situation in the coal industry is of particular interest. In 1873 the combined strength of the miners' unions stood at over 200,000, and there were two national organisations in existence. The National Miners' Association had been founded by Alexander Macdonald in 1863, and was a loose federal body. It covered Northumberland, Durham, Yorkshire, Scotland and parts of the Midlands. Its rival was the Amalgamated Association of Miners, formed in 1869 and led by Thomas Halliday. The Amalgamated was a centralised organisation, committed to a vigorous policy of action directed from the centre. It covered Lancashire, South Wales and the West Midlands.

Now, as Clegg, Fox and Thompson have emphasised, the unions in the coal industry – and this also applied to the iron and cotton industries – were placed in a very different situation from the craft societies. As we have seen, once these latter unions were firmly established, they could enforce their trade policies by a combination of unilateral action and localised collective bargaining, and so avoid large-scale clashes with employers.

> Unions in coal, cotton, and iron, however, had to face organised groups of employers, some of which were already settling wages and conditions over wide sections of their industries. These unions were therefore almost inevitably driven into extensive strikes. According to the imperfect records at our disposal there were eighteen stoppages between 1817 and 1889 in which more than a million 'working days' were lost. Nine of these were in mining, four in cotton, three in iron, and one in chain-making. Only one, among shipbuilding trades on the Clyde, affected any of the major craft societies; but the rapid fluctuations of activity in the shipyards posed problems for the Boilermakers which other societies did not share [19 :43].

As long as prices were rising the coal miners' unions prospered, but when in 1874 prices began to fall rapidly the unions were faced by concerted demands from the employers for wage decreases. Inevitably, the union response was usually one of resistance, and prolonged stoppages occurred in a number of coalfields. The results were disastrous for organisation, and Halliday's Amalgamated Association was dissolved in 1875.

There were, however, exceptions to the general ruin. The Northumberland and Durham miners' unions under the leadership of Burt and Crawford survived in strength, their combined membership dropping only from 56,000 in 1875 to 41,000 in 1880, and recovering to 48,000 by 1885 [19:19]. It is the contention of Clegg et al. that these unions survived because their leaders were ready to accept the principle that wage rates must fluctuate with prices, and in the last resort were prepared to embody that acceptance in the form of sliding-scale agreements with employers. These writers believe that the same point held true in the iron industry, where the men's organisation had largely collapsed at the end of the 1860s as a result of prolonged stoppages over wage cuts, but where an island of stability existed in the North East. Here John Kane of the Ironworkers had established a Conciliation Board with the employers, and this regulated wage changes in response to price movements. The Webbs interpreted union acceptance of sliding scales and similar arrangements in ideological terms: 'we see', they wrote, 'the sturdy leaders of many Trade Union battles gradually and insensibly accepting the capitalists' axiom that wages must necessarily fluctuate according to the capitalists' profits . . .' [68 :*339*] Clegg *et al.* saw the issue in a different light.

> But had Burt, Crawford and Kane not accepted the wage–price link during the seventies there would have been no unions of any strength in either industry a decade later. A recognition of the need for wage reductions was a condition of union survival at that time; and their sliding-scale agreements show a realisation that automatic adjustments through the formal machinery of the boards were to be preferred to the frontal clashes which had destroyed so many unions in the two industries [19 :*23*].

In this view, the moderate union leaders are seen as realists who calculated that unionism would not survive unless it was flexible in its attitude to wages.

Not all modern labour historians share this viewpoint. V. L. Allen has argued that the introduction of conciliation and arbitration procedures retarded the growth of unionism in the coal and iron industries. 'Where conciliation and arbitration were employed and were succeeded by sliding-scale agreements, trade unionism was contained and disarmed at a significant stage of its growth. To this extent the advocates of the formal institutional treatment of industrial disputes succeeded where the document, lockouts, and repressive legislation had failed' [1 :*82*]. Porter, writing on the same theme, believed that Allen had overstated his case, but felt that conciliation procedures may well have restricted union activity, although he saw these constraints as operating more particularly in the period after 1896 [60].

The issue is a complex one, but Allen's argument is by no means convincing. Writing of sliding-scale agreements, he comments :

> The consequence for trade unionism was that with an automatic means of regulating wages, trade unions became, or so it seemed at the time, largely unnecessary. After the introduction of the sliding scale in the South Wales coalfield, trade unionism died for about two decades . . . The introduction of sliding-scale agreements was one of the factors which caused the membership of the Association of Ironworkers to decline from 35,000 in 1873 to 1,400 in 1879 [1 : *81*].

Regarding the last point, it can equally well be argued that but for the Association's agreement with the employers in the North East it would have ceased to have any members. In any case between 1880 and 1890 the union's membership doubled, with the sliding scales still in operation [19 : *205*]. The point relating to South Wales is most misleading. Independent unions were destroyed in the South Wales coalfield in the lock-out of 1875, and sliding scales were introduced by the employers in conjunction with a system of company unionism. The position in the Northumberland and Durham coalfields, and in the iron industry of the same region, was quite different since here the sliding scale and conciliation board agreements involved the participation of independent unions that were certainly not in the pockets of the employers.

Allen does not in fact produce any clear evidence to show that sliding-scale agreements rendered unions 'largely unnecessary'. As Porter has pointed out, wage adjustments under sliding scales were not entirely automatic in character because there were time-limits to the scales' operation. 'If a scale was normally drawn up for two or three years it casts doubts on the view . . . that the unions were left functionless and that sliding scales were *per se* destructive of trade unionism. Since at the end of the three years the scale must be renegotiated, renewed, or rejected, there was a definite function left for the union' [60 : *467–8*]. On balance

then it seems likely that conciliation boards and agreements link-
ing wages and selling-prices aided rather than hindered union
survival after 1874.

In most coalfields unionism fared badly in the late seventies,
but mining unionism was nothing if not resilient. When prices
began to rise again in the early 1880s organisation revived, and
a forward move was possible once more. The early eighties saw
one very important development. As Clegg *et al.* have pointed
out, a weakness in each of the national organisations of the early
seventies was that they included both coalfields serving the home
market and those producing for export [19:20]. Price fluctuations were wider in the latter areas than in the former. A realign-
ment now began to take place. The main exporting areas –
Northumberland, Durham and South Wales – were all covered
by sliding-scale arrangements, albeit of differing kinds; and so
concerted activity for a general wage increase in 1882 was
confined to the so-called Central Coalfields – those producing
for the home market [2:64–5]. The movement achieved considerable success, but the new alliance was not put on a permanent footing. In the subsequent depression of 1885–7 the unions
were forced back on to the defensive, and concerted action was
abandoned. The experiment had, however, pointed the way to
the future, and when a forward movement again became
possible in 1888 it was repeated, and this time resulted in the
formation of the Miners' Federation of Great Britain [2:94–5].

So much for the miners. What of the fate of the thousands of
other non-craft unionists who had swelled the ranks of the movement in the early seventies? The period after 1875 is usually
seen as one of total defeat for the new sectors of organisation.
In general they did of course fare badly, although none worse
than agriculture where effective unionism had virtually ceased
to exist by the late eighties. However, some of the new unions
survived, even though their strength may have been much
diminished. The Amalgamated Society of Railway Servants
was one of these survivors and had 15,000 members in 1888.
The teachers' union of 1870 survived and prospered, claiming
over 14,000 members in 1888. In the wholesale boot and shoe
trade, the National Union of Operative Boot and Shoe Rivet-

ters and Finishers (later the National Union of Boot and Shoe Operatives), founded in 1874, survived and claimed 19,000 members in 1888. There were other new unions which did not perish. Of course, there were many casualties after 1874–5, but the dissolution of unions with the onset of depression did not always mean a cessation of all activity until 1889. The port industry provides a case in point. Taplin, in his study of dockers and seamen in Liverpool, has shown how, following the failure of the union established in 1872, the dockers established another organisation in 1880 – this developed out of a large-scale strike movement in 1879 [66]. In a similar study, Brown has drawn attention to the Hull dock strike of 1879 which was followed in 1881 by a much larger stoppage, involving dockers and seamen, and resulting in a revival of organisation [12]. As there was also a dock strike in London in 1880, it appears that there was a good deal of activity taking place in the ports during the up-swing of trade after 1879. It could well be the case that in a number of other industries unions which collapsed in the later seventies were revived after 1879, even if only for a short period.

Finally, the period 1875–88 witnessed not merely survivals and revivals, but some new creations as well. Most notable among these latter was John Hodge's British Steel Smelters' Amalgamated Association, founded in 1886. This union, which began in Scotland but quickly spread into England and Wales, rapidly absorbed workers in the expanding steel industry – workers that the Association of Ironworkers had not bothered to organise. Hodge's union had a dynamic and controversial future ahead of it. The same year, 1886, also saw the formation of the important Card and Blowing Room Operatives union in the cotton industry.

It has been argued above that the period 1875–88 was not as moribund as has sometimes been claimed. It cannot be denied, however, that the industrial movement failed to consolidate many of its earlier gains, and that with 750,000 members in 1888, as against perhaps one million or more in 1874, it had lost ground over the period. The figure of 750,000 represented only 10 per cent of all adult male manual workers in the country

16

[19 :*1–2*]. Cole attributed unionism's setback to the 'Great Depression', but the whole notion of such a depression covering the years 1873–96 has been discredited; Saul concluded his study of the subject with the words : 'the sooner the "Great Depression" is banished from the literature, the better' [64 :*55*]. The truth was that unionism had benefited from quite exceptionally favourable economic conditions in the early 1870s, when unemployment was remarkably low. It was not to be expected that these boom conditions would persist indefinitely, nor that they would be repeated quickly, and some falling off in membership was inevitable.

General economic factors apart, however, unionism during this period, and for long afterwards, suffered from a fundamental difficulty : its inability to absorb on a permanent basis the mass of lower-paid workers in industries where it had secured a foothold. It was H. A. Turner who first gave this problem the serious attention which it deserves. In his study of the cotton unions he noted how most unions in the nineteenth century originated from informal groups of workers possessing a sense of sectional solidarity [67]. In theory such groups could have formed the cores around which larger organisations could have developed, bringing in the mass of workers who possessed no established sectional solidarities. In practice, however, they mostly adopted a form of unionism 'that not merely gave no encouragement to the growth of trade unionism in *general*, but actively discouraged it' [67 :*180–1*]. This form Turner described as 'closed' unionism. Closed unions deliberately restricted entry to the occupation they organised, and their bargaining power hinged upon this restriction. They were not interested in expansion outside of their narrow sectional boundaries since they did not depend on size for strength.

Turner believed that in the spinning section of the cotton industry the prior organisation of the key workers in closed unions stultified the general development of unionism in that sector during the second half of the nineteenth century. By contrast, the early establishment of 'open' weavers' unions in the manufacturing side of the industry stimulated the development of unionism throughout that section of the industry. Open unions of the kind developed by the weavers were, however, unusual in the mid-nineteenth century, and Turner argued that in most industries outside cotton the situation approximated to that in the spinning section, with entrenched closed unions stultifying the general development of unionism.

It is not possible to subject Turner's thesis to detailed scrutiny in this study, but there can be no doubt that his contribution is an important one. The precise nature of the situation tended to vary from industry to industry, but everywhere there was the basic problem of extending unionism from a privileged group to the mass.

In industries in which strong craft unions existed – engineering, shipbuilding, printing, building – the position was fairly clear-cut; established unions catered only for apprenticed workers or their equivalents. In cotton, mining, iron and steel and transport – industries without an apprenticeship system – things were more fluid, although in iron the union was actually composed of contractors who employed the less-skilled workers. In mining the unions tended to absorb the mass of workers during periods of prosperity, but in periods of weakness all but the better-paid faceworkers dropped away and the unions even began to exhibit a tendency to consolidate around the faceworkers alone. It was this situation that was at the root of one of the bitterest coal strikes of this period – the 1881 dispute in Lancashire. In the later seventies only the faceworkers had remained organised in Lancashire, and they ran the union as their own. With improving trade in 1881, however, a strike broke out in which the non-unionist day-wage men took the lead. The union had no control whatever over these men who ran the strike committee and employed violent tactics to such effect that soldiers were brought in to restore order. The experience was an extremely salutary one for the union, and in the years that followed it made strenuous efforts to organise the lower-paid workers in order to obtain control of the situation [14 : *164–79, 202–4*]. In the docks the situation was rather similar to mining – in London at any rate – with the unions tending to consolidate around the better-paid stevedores, corn porters and lightermen, and the mass of dockers drifting out of organisation [41 : *ch.* 3].

18

Although there were union leaders who realised the undesirability of this situation, it was not easy to combat it. Better-paid workers in mining, the docks and, of course, in craft industries were deeply prejudiced against the lower-paid workers, and these in their turn resented the exclusiveness of established unionism. Lower-paid workers, furthermore, were not easily absorbed into unions even when these were open in theory. Such workers were often employed on a casual basis and exhibited all the well-known characteristics of casual workers. That this was not a problem confined to the docks emerges clearly from Fox's description of the outworkers in the boot and shoe trade of the seventies. Referring to the 'protracted problems with which the new infant union had to grapple', he drew attention to 'the isolation and low bargaining power of the outworker; his addiction, nevertheless, to the redeeming factor of independence and freedom from authority and discipline; the recurrent recklessness encouraged by this mode of working life; the trade customs and petty embezzlements which it made possible and which soured the manufacturer towards outworkers as a body; and, above all, the ease of entry into the trade' [31 : 26].

Thus many lower-paid workers had neither the resources nor the inclination to attach themselves to trade unions, and in any case many unions were none too keen to receive them. An imponderable factor in all this was the role of the employers. Employers were sometimes prepared to deal with unions composed of the better-paid and more respectable of their manual employees while at the same time refusing to tolerate unionism amongst the rest. One may only guess at the extent to which this factor acted as a deterrent to the extension of unionism.

2 *1889 – Socialism and New Unionism*

ACCORDING to Cole, 1889 was the year in which 'British Labour' asserted itself 'as a movement of the whole labour class against exploitation' [23]. Other labour historians who have written from a socialist standpoint have likewise seen 1889 as a great turning-point in the history of the movement. What made this year so significant for these writers was not so much the great increase in trade union membership, as the influence gained by socialism in the trade union world. The Webbs wrote : 'Within a decade [from 1885] we find the whole Trade Union world permeated with Collectivist ideas. . . . This revolution in opinion is the chief event of Trade Union history at the close of the nineteenth century' [68 : *374–5*]. Various modern writers have made the same basic point. Thus E. J. Hobsbawm suggested : 'Ideologically and politically the union expansions after 1889 marked a sharp turn to the left, the creation of a new cadre of leaders and policy-makers – mostly inspired by various versions of socialism – and the association of the movement with an independent working-class political party and, after 1918, a socialist programme' [35 : *358*].

For writers such as these socialism constituted the keystone of the union movement. In its absence during the sixties, seventies and much of the eighties, unions were divided amongst themselves because there was 'no coherent ideological basis for unity : no reasoned case for heightening workingmen's consciousness in their class solidarity' [1 : *143*]. In this perspective, the conjunction of trade unionism and socialism was a natural and necessary event. Not all historians have taken this view. S. Perlman, an American, argued that socialism was an ideology that was essentially alien to mature trade unionism, but he has had few disciples in this country [56]. Perlman's viewpoint deserves more

20

attention, for even his opponents must concede that the conversion of British trade unionism to socialism was tardy and incomplete. In this chapter an attempt will be made to assess the impact of socialism upon the trade union world in the decade or so following 1889.

In the years 1889–91 total trade union membership doubled. This was a remarkable expansion, although possibly not an unprecedented one. The tendency for trade union membership to expand in sudden dramatic bursts is well known, and the upsurge of 1889–91 had been preceded by similar expansions in 1833–5 and 1872–4. Upheavals of this kind were by no means peculiar to Britain. Indeed, the 1880s in America witnessed a burst of union activity and links between that movement and the later British one have been suggested by Pelling [51]. Historians have long sought to explain this uneven pattern of trade union growth, and a whole range of theories have been advanced [10]. It seems reasonable to suggest, however, that socialism was not a cause of the upheaval of 1889. It is true of course that a socialist revival had taken place in the 1880s, and that members of the Social Democratic Federation had made the most of the heavy unemployment of 1884–7 in their efforts to win working class support. But the great union expansion coincided with the period of high employment running from 1889 to 1891. In this sense it was a repeat performance of the great upsurge of 1872–4 which had also occurred at a time of high employment. There was no mystery about this. In an overstocked labour market, such as existed in nineteenth-century Britain, it was only in times of exceptionally high employment that the mass of workers possessed any bargaining power. A socialist revival had not been necessary to trigger off the upsurge of the early seventies; there is no reason to assume that it was a factor in the late eighties. The significance of socialism hinges, then, upon its success in capturing a movement which it did not itself cause.

Hobsbawm has suggested that 'explosions' of the kind of 1889–91 are marked by qualitative as well as quantitative changes. 'They are, in fact, generally expansions of the movement into new industries, new regions, new classes of the population; they coincide with a clustering of new organisations, and the

21

adoption of new ideas and policies by both new and existing units' [34 : 127]. The year 1889 is remembered in particular for its new organisations – the New Unions. There had been new unions in 1872 and, like those of 1889, they had recruited among the mass of lower-paid and lesser-skilled workers. What was so special about the New Unions of 1889 ?

A basic point concerns their structure. As in the seventies the new organisations were a mixture; some were general in character, recruiting members wherever they could find them, others confined themselves to a particular industry or occupation. In the late eighties, however, the general unions were much more prominent than they had been in the earlier period. It is easy to assume that this prominence was a result of socialist influence because general unionism was certainly a congenial form of organisation to the socialist. It implied the essential solidarity of the mass of wage-earners, and was linked with aspirations towards the One Big Union of the whole working class [9 : 3–28]. Furthermore, given the contemporary notion that the mass of workers were simply labourers, mobile workers without roots in any particular industry, general unionism seemed the most practicable way of organising them [34 : 181]. Socialists were certainly active in these unions. Tom Mann, a member of the S.D.F., became President of the Dockers' Union which emerged out of the great London dock strike of 1889. Will Thorne, another S.D.F. man, was leader of the Gasworkers' and General Labourers' Union. These are the best known examples, but there are many others [53 : ch. 5].

The extent of socialist involvement in the general unions is not in doubt, but involvement is not the same thing as influence. Clegg *et al.* have argued that the prominence of the general unions was not a result of socialist influence. 'But socialist influence did not determine whether a "new union" became a "general union". Some of the organisations which they helped to set up, like the Gasworkers, did so; but others, like the Leeds Builders' Labourers . . . did not. Similarly, not all the unions which were or became "general" owed much to the socialists' [19 : 91]. The view of Clegg *et al.* was that the major general unions adopted this form uninten-

22

tionally. 'Setting out to cater for a particular group of workers – gasworkers, dockers, or shipyard labourers – they found other workers clamouring to join and let them in' [19:92]. It was, however, in all probability the influence of the socialists within the Gasworkers' Union which encouraged it to maintain its character as a purely open union, whereas some other general unions exhibited early on a tendency towards exclusiveness. This tendency arose because the unions quickly discovered that their membership was not after all composed of a shifting mass of labourers but of numerous sections of workers each possessing strong links with one particular branch of employment [34:184]. Many of these groups quickly learnt to use their unions to protect their own spheres of employment from the intrusion of outsiders.

Whether they were general unions or not, the organisations established in 1889 were long believed by labour historians to be notable for their 'adoption of new ideas and policies'. Cole wrote :

In most cases, the 'New' Unions dispensed with friendly benefits altogether, and concentrated on the possession of funds for use in strikes and lock-outs and in the expenses of organising and administration. Their leaders denounced friendly benefits as leading to stagnation and reaction in industrial policy. They set out to build up Unions which would be able to appeal to the entire working class, and to follow a fighting policy based on class solidarity and directed, by implication at any rate, against the capitalist system itself. In short, the 'New' Unions were in intention Socialist . . . [24:246].

In recent years, however, some historians have been inclined to question this picture. It is of course true that contemporary socialists, both inside and outside the unions, liked to think of them as militant, free from friendly benefits, open, class-conscious and socialist. But Clegg et al. believe that this image is not borne out by the facts; the new unions simply did not conform to a set pattern [19:92–6]. Some were led by socialists, but others were not. Some adopted militant postures, others pursued con-

23

ciliatory policies from the beginning. Some introduced friendly benefits at the outset, others later on.

In drawing attention to these things Clegg *et al.* are doing more than simply stating the facts of the matter; they are, as Hobsbawm has pointed out, putting forward an interpretation of trade union history that is different from that usually advanced by labour historians. 'Their argument is . . . that effective trade union policy had nothing to do with ideological views or the formal organisational structures purporting to reflect them, but consisted essentially in the realistic calculation of tactical possibilities and bargaining strengths . . . within a fixed framework of industrial relations' [35:*360*]. Thus, the structure and policies of the new unions of 1889 were, in their view, determined not by ideology, but by the requirements of survival in differing industrial contexts. Certainly research carried out into the nature of waterside unionism in this period, indicating a continuity between the older and newer organisations so far as their basic objectives were concerned, lends support to the view of Clegg *et al.* [41]. The 'industrial relations' approach of these writers does not, however, find favour with Hobsbawm. Even so, the latter's own characterisation of the general unions, as 'offspring of a marriage between the class unionism of the socialists and the more modest plans of the unskilled themselves', suggests a limited role for socialist ideology [34:*182*].

Survival was the basic problem for the new organisations. They were assailed by attacks from the employers even before the trade boom had subsided, and once the downswing did commence in 1891 they were pushed even further on the defensive. Whatever may be said of their qualities at the time of their foundation, there can be little disagreement as to the direction of their development after the boom was over. It was Hobsbawm who referred to general unionism in the years 1892–1910 as 'cautious, limited and conservative "sectional" unionism' [34:*191*]. The new organisations lost thousands of members in the early nineties, but as institutions they showed considerable resilience, and of the major new creations only the seamen collapsed altogether.

General unionism proved to be an effective form of organisa-

24

tion because it facilitated the task of survival. It enabled the unions to 'spread their risks between industries and areas not all of which were liable to attack at the same time' [34:*192*]. None the less it is clear that a critical factor in the survival of all the new organisations, general or otherwise, was employer recognition. Where this could not be obtained, or was withdrawn, organisation generally collapsed. This happened in many of the ports. The Dockers' Union lost nearly all its membership among the dockers of London and Hull, but was enabled to survive as an institution largely because of its foothold in the tinplate industry of South Wales where it was recognised by the employers. The National Amalgamated Union of Labour, another general union, obtained a secure foothold among the labourers in the shipyards of the North East again because in this sphere it enjoyed employer recognition. Hobsbawm noted : 'Clearly, the class-conscious militancy of the early leaders was less likely to commend itself in such a state of affairs than a more cautious and conciliatory policy' [34:*189*]. Unions established in the early seventies, such as the National Union in the boot and shoe trade, had depended for their continued existence upon employer acceptance; so it was with the organisations of 1889. In so far as new organisations were able to survive without recognition, there is some evidence to suggest that friendly benefits were a critical factor in keeping the membership together : a circumstance not without its irony [36:*33–4*].

Those historians who have emphasised the role of socialism in the union expansion of 1889–91 have pointed out that its influence extended beyond the new unions; new ideas and policies were adopted by 'both new and existing units' [34:*127*]. The existing units are important, for their membership also grew during the expansion, and in numerical terms they entirely dominated the movement. The combined strength of the new unions in 1892 has been estimated at about 200,000, whereas the figure for total membership in that year – the first, incidentally, for which we have an official estimate – was 1·5 millions. By 1900 the new unions accounted for less than one-tenth of all trade unionists [19:*97*]. The craft unions in engineering, shipbuilding, printing and building; the Miners' Federation, whose

25

membership was to be increased enormously at the end of the nineties as a result of the revival of mining unionism in Scotland and Wales; and the cotton unions – these were the three bastions of unionism in the two decades after 1889. How strong was the influence of socialism in this sector?

It was Tom Mann who observed: 'There is as large a proportion of carpenters, masons, engineers, and cotton operatives avowed Socialists, as is to be found amongst the gas workers, dockers, chemical workers and general labourers' [19:294]. The implication was that the old unions as much as the new were influenced by socialism, and, as Pelling has pointed out, there was a certain logic to this situation. It was, after all, much more likely that socialism would appeal to better-paid workers who formed the existing unions than to unskilled men, simply because the former 'were more literate and so more open to rational or quasi-rational argument' [55:18], and this judgement is confirmed by the social surveys of Mayhew and Booth [55:56–61]. Within the established unions it was in all probability the younger men who were particularly attracted to socialism, whereas the ageing union leaderships tended to cling to the Radical Liberal ideology which they had acquired in their youth. As Asa Briggs has remarked: 'there is real value in labour history, as in other branches of history, in thinking in terms of generations' [11:3]. In time, the socialist rebels of the nineties would become the trade union establishment.

Hobsbawm has suggested that the new socialist ideology 'attracted a quite extraordinary number and proportion of union activists': a view obtained by contrasting the large number of socialists among leading union functionaries by 1900 with the 'derisory' membership of the socialist political societies at that time [35:361]. In his view this success of socialism was a result of its relevance. Union activists seized on socialism because it provided an analysis of the contemporary industrial situation which was more realistic than the 'commonplaces of economic liberalism' [35:362].

Hobsbawm cites two examples. First, the 1890s witnessed considerable technical change in a number of industries, change which threatened the status of the craftsman. Against this background, the Marxian argument that mechanisation reduced the skilled to the ranks of the unskilled carried conviction. Secondly, the socialist theory of capitalist concentration also appeared relevant when the organisations of the employers were advancing apace, and inflicting some severe defeats on the unions, as in the Hull dock strike of 1893 and the great engineering lock-out of 1897. Furthermore, the idea of capitalist concentration suggested that the unions in their turn should seek to co-ordinate their activities and merge into larger units. In this sense 'socialism became a potential programme of modernisation for trade unions' [35 : *362*]. In reality, the concentration of capital had not proceeded very far in Britain at this time; but, as Pelling has shown, British unionists were well aware of the American experience, where the trust system developed rapidly and culminated in the formation of the United States Steel Corporation in 1901. 'It was widely assumed that the existing state of America reflected the future state of Britain, and that the existing state of America was an unhappy one for the worker. Although both these assumptions were at least partially mistaken, they did their work' [52 : *88*].

If socialism did indeed become 'a potential programme of modernisation for trade unions', the crucial test as to its influence is the extent to which modernisation was in fact carried out. Hobsbawm saw the process as continuing beyond 1900 into the mid-1920s, but even by this latter date relatively little had been achieved. Some unions had grown very much larger as a result of amalgamations but a large number of small units remained, and trade union structure as a whole had certainly not become more rational – proposals to reorganise the movement on the basis of industrial unionism were buried at the T.U.C. conference of 1927 [42 : *99–101*]. The efforts that had been made to co-ordinate trade union action had ended in disaster. Hobsbawm himself was forced to conclude 'that the systematic adaptation of the movement to twentieth-century technology, business structure, and industrial organisation which the "new unionism" recommended, did not achieve its object' [35 : *363*]. Socialism failed to break down the sectionalism of the unions.

But the influence of the socialists was in any case ambiguous so far as the process of modernisation was concerned. In the craft industries in the late nineteenth century the unions were threatened by the introduction of new machinery – machinery that was manned by semi-skilled workers. The response of the national leaderships of the craft unions was, in general, to seek to open up the ranks of the unions to these new categories of worker. This was a policy that accorded well with the socialist analysis of the situation, and indeed socialists were prominent in some of the attempts to implement it. The rank and file, however, invariably resisted such moves, and sought to maintain the exclusiveness of the craft societies. This happened in the 1890s and 1900s in the Tailors', the Engineers', the Boilermakers' and a number of other craft unions [19 : ch. 4].

The obstinacy of the rank and file on this issue was part of a general resistance to the encroachments made by new technology on craft status, and the discontent of the craftsmen was directed against both the employers and the national union leaderships. Before long, socialists were to be found at the head of the revolt; and, as Clegg *et al.* have pointed out, a rather extraordinary situation then emerged.

Among the Engineers, as among the Boot and Shoe Operatives, the socialists had increased their influence by putting themselves in the forefront of an aggressive industrial movement to resist technical and organisational change. Thus socialists intent on pursuing the class war to end all privilege allied themselves with members anxious to preserve their ancient privileges against the inroads of machines, piece-work, and unskilled workers [19 : *297*].

The role of the socialists in relation to technical change – and therefore to modernisation – was ambiguous. This was so before the First World War, and it was to become particularly apparent during the war itself.

If the impact of socialism on the structure and policies of the industrial movement proved to be limited, even in the long run, it none the less appears that the socialist revival made a fundamental difference in the political sphere, for at the end of the century the unions were at last drawn into a political alliance with the socialist societies, and so the Labour Party was born. The extent to which this development marked a major ideological shift in the trade union world will be examined in the next chapter.

3 Taff Vale

IT is possible to interpret the decision of the unions to participate in a political alliance with the socialist societies as stemming
from a fundamental reappraisal of their position in society. The
socialists could, and did, point to a range of developments taking
place in the 1890s which indicated the hostility of the ruling class
to labour: employer organisation, adverse legal decisions and
the concentration of capital and weakness of unionism in the
United States. In the face of this evidence many even of the old
guard of union leaders began to accept parts of the socialist case,
as Clegg *et al.* have noted [19:*304*]. Some labour historians
of the socialist school have indeed argued that the period 1889–
1900 did witness in reality a general reaction of the governing
class against labour, so that the socialist propaganda of the time
was no more than the truth. The most important contribution
of this kind is that by J. Saville [63].

Saville argued that the series of adverse decisions against the
unions in the Courts from the mid-nineties down to 1901 – the
year of the Taff Vale decision – formed part and parcel of a
general reaction against trade unionism in general and new
unionism in particular. 'This whole period after 1889 is one of
developing counter-attack by the propertied classes against the
industrial organisations of the working people' [63:*317*].
Focusing on the waterfront, Saville was able to show how the
initial goodwill of the public at the time of the 1889 dock strike
quickly faded away to be replaced by hostile denunciations of
the new unions in the press, and the mobilisation of contingents
of strike-breakers by virulently anti-union employers. In particular, the reliance of the new waterside unions upon heavy picket-
ing during disputes called down the wrath of employers and
'respectable' public opinion; and from the early nineties on-

ward the government countered this tactic by the use of large police and military forces. 'When, as from the middle years of the decade, the decisions of the Courts began to echo the hostility of the employers and the prejudice of the politicians towards trade unionism, the working men found themselves in a world in which their accepted position was being rapidly undermined' [63 : *341*]. Thus, in classic Marxist fashion, the employers, the judiciary and the state are seen as reacting vigorously to the pretensions of the organised workers. The culminating event in this prolonged capitalist counter-offensive was the Taff Vale decision of 1901 which determined that trade unions could be sued for damages caused by the actions of their officers. This decision was described by Saville as the 'final breakthrough' [63 : *317*].

Historians have long agreed that the Taff Vale decision was of critical importance in securing union support for the alliance with the socialist societies; because, although the Labour Representation Committee had been set up in 1900, it was not until after Taff Vale that the Committee won widespread support among the unions. Thus, in Saville's perspective, the capitalist counter-offensive led directly to the formation of the new labour alliance. In so far as Saville's interpretation of the nineties as a period of wholesale reaction against trade unionism is accurate, it would seem entirely probable that the conversion of the unions to independent labour representation reflected a fundamental reappraisal of their situation : an acceptance, in fact, of the socialist analysis of industrial society. But is Saville's interpretation accurate?

Leaving aside the legal position for a moment, it is of course true that many employers adopted an extreme anti-union position, particularly on the waterfront, but in other spheres as well. At the time of the 1897 engineering lock-out anti-union feeling ran very high. However, Clegg *et al.* have questioned how general this reaction was.

Had British employers wished to be rid of trade unions, the depression years of 1902–5, with the Taff Vale precedent valid in every court, were as favourable an opportunity as ever

31

presented itself. There are, however, relatively few instances of organised employers taking advantage of it to attempt to weaken or destroy the unions . . . This can be taken as evidence that most employers were not 'anti-union' [19:*362–3*].

Reviewing the whole period covered by their volume, they note that already by 1889 the area of employer recognition of trade unions was quite extensive, covering nearly all craft trades, cotton, iron and steel, and some coalfields. By 1910 this area of recognition had been extended 'over a far wider range of industry than in 1889' [19:*484*].

In view of this situation it is surely not possible to regard Taff Vale as the 'final breakthrough' in a sustained capitalist offensive. It is possible, certainly, to argue that, although the decision was not followed by a final onslaught, the unions were none the less critically weakened by it, and that this weakness showed itself in the absence of widespread strike activity during the opening years of the new century. Phelps Brown, for example, thought that the effect of the judgement on the unions was 'overwhelming' and suggested that 'the impression was strong and the threat real that any strike would result in the union's funds being mulcted'; consequently 'there were few strikes' [57:*194–5*]. This view, however, has also been questioned by Clegg et al. They point out that 'the period during which the Taff Vale judgement exerted its full effect on annual strike statistics consisted at most only of the four years from 1902 to 1905'; whereas 'the period of industrial peace lasted nine years' – 1899–1907 [19:*327*]. They therefore suggest that there were other important influences at work restraining strike activity.

It was the decline of working days lost in the three great industries of cotton, coal mining and engineering and shipbuilding, which was the critical factor in the period. Clegg et al. attribute this decline to the relatively successful operation of the collective bargaining procedures that had been set up in these industries during the 1890s, following a series of severe stoppages [19:*362*]. More generally, these authors point to the willingness of the majority of organised employers to work with the

32

unions, and cite the example of the building industry where the employers strengthened and extended the system of collective bargaining [19 :*363*]. Thus, while Taff Vale may not have been without effect, there appear to have been more positive influences making for industrial peace.

It appears, then, that on the industrial front the period 1889–1901 did not in fact witness a widespread breakdown in union–employer relations. It did, however, see major new developments in these relations in a number of industries: developments which were to continue well into the new century. The analysis by Clegg *et al.* ascribes to technical change the main spur to development. As we noted in an earlier chapter, the craft unions traditionally sought to control working conditions through action at local level – either by means of unilateral regulation or by collective bargaining with employers on a town or district basis. As the rate of technical change increased, however, craft controls became increasingly unacceptable to employers, and in order to break through them they began to form associations, just as the employers in coal, cotton and iron had formed organisations in order to regulate conditions in their respective industries. The craft unions could thus no longer pick off one firm or town at a time; they now had to deal with employers collectively. As Clegg *et al.* have pointed out, however, this development was not entirely unwelcome within the various craft societies. To the national leaderships there was some advantage to be gained by dealing with employers' organisations. It enhanced their authority within the union and made it possible to negotiate necessary changes centrally rather than wasting the union's resources in a series of local disputes over which they had no control [19 :*169*]. To the branches, on the other hand, it meant a reduction in local autonomy. Of course, leadership and branches often found themselves united in resisting the employers' challenge, as during the engineering lock-out of 1897. But out of such struggles collective bargaining machinery often emerged which the leadership was more ready to accept than the rank and file. Thus, as Clegg *et al.* observe: 'Some of the national agreements represented a joint victory for employers and trade union leaders over the hostility of a rank and file which was still wedded to the traditions of unilateral regulation' [19 : *471*].

The growth of collective bargaining was thus inseparably bound up with the struggle within the unions between centralisation and local autonomy. Although the struggle was most intense in the craft industries because of the traditional method of functioning of the craft unions, it was found in other industries as well. In the work of Clegg *et al.* the interrelated problems of employer organisation, union centralisation and rank and file resistance crop up again and again. A wide range of industries were affected – engineering, printing, cotton spinning, boots and shoes, tailoring, shipbuilding, building – although of course the exact manner in which these problems were resolved varied greatly from industry to industry.

In the above analysis the employers' challenge appears as a rather more complex phenomenon than Saville suggested. It was a challenge which divided the unions internally rather than united them. We now turn to the role of the Courts.

It is perhaps not surprising that the series of legal judgements adversely affecting the status of the unions that culminated in Taff Vale should have been seen, both at the time and subsequently, as part of an all-embracing attack on unionism. Yet there is no evidence that these decisions formed part of a concerted plan, and the judges did not always decide against the unions [19 : *307*]. Furthermore, the Taff Vale decision itself was not simply a reflection of judicial hostility to unionism; it was also related, as Pelling has observed, to developments in legal procedure outside the field of industrial relations – in particular to the development of the device known as the 'representative action' [55 : *72, 80*]. Most important of all is the fact that the trade union reaction to Taff Vale was a divided one [8 : *ch.* 4; 19 : *ch.* 8].

Within the trade union world there was in certain quarters an inclination to accept the judgement as a positive development, provided certain safeguards could be obtained. Indeed, the Bill promoted by the T.U.C. Parliamentary Committee, and brought before Parliament in 1903, contained a clause ruling out actions for damages against a union *only* in cases where members had acted without union authority. In the event the clause had to be dropped for technical reasons and the truncated Bill was defeated, but when a new and tougher measure was proposed at the 1903 Trade Union Congress, seeking to restore to the unions complete immunity, an amendment was moved in favour of the original policy. This was defeated and a harder line definitely adopted, but the existence of a not inconsiderable body of trade union opinion which favoured acceptance of union liability is of some interest.

As Pelling has pointed out, the divisions within the movement over the response to Taff Vale cannot be wholly explained in terms of clashing ideologies [55 : 80]. It is true that the socialists provided the most ardent advocates of a complete return to the pre-Taff Vale situation, and that some of those who opposed this line were 'Lib-Labs' who saw acceptance of union liability as a means of strengthening union discipline and keeping in check the militant socialists among the rank and file. But socialists were also to be found among the strong supporters of union liability, while there were many 'Lib-Labs' who took the opposite view.

This situation reflected in part a genuine uncertainty in the minds of trade unionists as to the best policy to adopt. But, more important, it reflected the varying industrial needs of the different unions. In so far as it is possible to generalise, it was the case that those unions which had secured recognition from the employers were the least inclined to become involved with the law, whereas those unions which remained unrecognised sought the law's assistance. Pelling has shown how this distinction operated clearly in the debate in trade union circles on the desirability of compulsory arbitration of industrial disputes. Ben Tillett, whose Dockers' Union had been broken in the ports by anti-union employers, first moved a resolution (at the 1899 T.U.C.) in favour of compulsory arbitration – which would force employers to deal with the unions – and he persisted in his advocacy of this scheme at subsequent Congresses, though without success. 'On each occasion he secured support from the leaders of other unions which had not won the employers' recognition, such as the Railway Servants, the Shop Assistants and the Postal Telegraph Clerks. But he had to face the scepticism of the unions which had already achieved a satisfactory bargaining status, such as the Miners, the Boilermakers, and the Compositors' [55:74]. The socialist Tillett and the 'Lib-Lab' Richard Bell – leader of the Railway Servants – were both prepared to accept union liability after Taff Vale, even though Bell's union was the one directly affected by the decision, because they saw it as a necessary step towards legally enforceable agreements and hence compulsory arbitration [8:81; 19:319].

In the event, the tide swung against Tillett and his associates because most union leaders, whatever their ideological persuasion, came to feel that close involvement with the law would bring more loss than gain: a conclusion that owed much to the scale of damages and costs awarded against the railway union in the case that followed the original Taff Vale decision [19:323]. Pelling has suggested that 1903, when the policy of acceptance of union liability finally foundered at the T.U.C., was a decisive turning-point for British industrial relations: 'The strong unions had won the day for the policy of complete freedom from the law; and as the weaker unions came also to be strong, they accepted this attitude' [55:79]. In 1906 the Trade Disputes Act passed by the Liberal Government embodied the policy in legislation. In no sense, however, did this represent a victory for socialism. It simply ensured the survival of a voluntary system of industrial relations in which there was as much scope for sectionalism as socialism.

Trade union leaders recognised the importance of the Taff Vale decision from the outset, although opinions were divided as to the remedy. It does not appear, however, that they regarded the case as part of a massive attack on their position, and the situation in industry certainly did not suggest that such a threat existed. It seems unlikely, therefore, that union support for the Labour Representation Committee came as a result of a fundamental reappraisal of the situation, or that it entailed a major ideological shift. Most trade union leaders simply had in view the urgent need to achieve a satisfactory legal status for the movement.

36

There remains, however, the question as to why they felt it necessary to go outside the established political parties – the Liberal Party in particular – in order to achieve this object. In his study of the origins of the Labour Party, Pelling has argued that the Liberals themselves were partly responsible for this development [53]. The chief political concern of the trade unions – apart, of course, from the legal issue – was to obtain more working-class Members of Parliament. The electoral reforms of the 1880s had stimulated union efforts in this direction, but since that time the Liberal Party had let down its trade union supporters in two critical respects.

In the first place the official Liberal Party constituency caucuses failed to adopt working men as candidates on any considerable scale, despite the favourable attitude of the party's leaders. The situation was analogous to that in the craft unions where the branches refused to widen the basis of membership despite the efforts of union leaders to persuade them to do so. Secondly, the Liberal Party failed to press for the payment of Members of Parliament, a vital consideration in working-class candidatures. Pelling has suggested that if this reform had been 'carried or at least urgently pressed by the 1892–5 Liberal government, it might have removed a main factor in the support given by the smaller unions to the idea of a separate Labour Party' [53 :224]. The discontent with the Liberal record in this respect may also help to explain why 'Lib-Lab' trade unionists offered such little resistance to the formation of the new party. This absence of resistance is noted by Clegg *et al.* who argue that the T.U.C. decision which led to the formation of the Labour Representation Committee could be attributed 'as much to the fact that the Lib-Labs did not organise its defeat as to the drive and political skills of the socialists' [19 :303].

Whatever the precise reasons for the setting up of the Committee, it is clear from subsequent events that this development had little ideological content. The new party functioned as little more than an adjunct of the Liberal Party, and in 1903 Ramsay MacDonald concluded on its behalf the famous electoral *entente* with that party [8: *ch.* 6]. Most of the trade union

37

leaders who joined the L.R.C. remained Liberals in all but name. Pelling has gone so far as to claim :

> They had no policy which was in advance of Liberalism; indeed, they tended to follow the Liberal lead rather than to force the pace in all matters except those directly affecting trade unions. It was in deference to their views that the Labour Party remained, in the years before the First World War, uncommitted, not merely to Socialism, but to any programme whatsoever [55 :*15*].

Although this may be putting the matter rather strongly, it was true that the L.R.C.'s 1906 election manifesto differed little from that of the Liberal Party. Furthermore, the success of the new party in that election was a success for Liberalism rather than Socialism, since the main electoral issues were free trade, education and the Chinese labour question [55 :*17;* 19 : *386–7*].

The liberalism of the Labour Party was reinforced in 1908–9 by the affiliation of the Miners, an event which prompted Bernard Shaw to remark, 'What then becomes of Socialism?' [55 :*16*]. The Miners were predominantly 'Lib-Lab' in sympathy during this period, and their affiliation certainly enhanced the discontent of the socialists within the party [19 :*410*]. The year 1909 also brought the Osborne judgement which had the effect of restraining unions from spending their funds for political purposes. The Webbs saw in this judgement simply another example of the prejudice of the governing class against both the industrial and political organisations of labour [68 :*608*]. It is more likely that, as Clegg *et al.* have suggested, it constituted the judicial reaction to the privileges conferred on the unions by the 1906 Trade Disputes Act [19 :*415*]. But the Osborne case has another and more interesting aspect, for it is clear that Osborne himself, the trade unionist who initiated the case, was no mere tool of the governing class. The Webbs suggested that he was financed by capitalists [68 :*608*]; but as Clegg *et al.* have pointed out : 'Osborne's support came from within the unions as well as from without', and the judgement 'was as much in favour of old-fashioned Lib-Labs and Conservative working men as of the ruling class and its alleged agents' [19 :*415*]. Osborne was a staunch unionist, but not a socialist, and he objected to his union enforcing a political levy in order to support a party which contained socialists amongst its membership. In this he was very far from being alone in the trade union world, and the chief officer of his own union, in fact, shared his viewpoint.

In the event, the labour movement had to wait until 1913 before the issue was resolved by Parliament. Under the provisions of the Trade Union Act passed in that year, any union wishing to engage in political activity had to secure a majority in favour of such action in a ballot of the membership. The results of these ballots showed the extent of the opposition to the labour alliance as late as 1913. Thus the Miners voted 261,643 for a political fund, 194,800 against; the Cotton Weavers, 98,158 for, 75,893 against [19 :*418n*].

In the long run it is of course arguable that the decision of the unions to participate in a political alliance with the socialist organisations led to profound changes in the nature of trade union political activity. In 1918 the Labour Party definitely adopted a socialist programme, and the trade unions were therefore committed in theory to the achievement of socialism. Important as this step was, it is possible to exaggerate the discontinuity between the pre-1914 Labour Party and the party of the 1918 socialist constitution. R. Harrison has argued that the socialist commitment did not in fact indicate the presence of a coherent ideology : 'It is better regarded as a rallying point around which the adherents of different ideologies and the representatives of different interests assembled' [32 :*259*].

Although trade union leaders increasingly talked the language of socialism, it is not always easy to see how this ideology actually influenced their behaviour in politics and industry. I. Richter indeed has gone so far as to claim that, despite appearances to the contrary, the fundamental political purposes of British unions have remained unmodified from the late nineteenth to the mid-twentieth centuries. In this view, the unions joined the Labour Party at the turn of the century in order to secure a legal framework which permitted free collective bargaining, and this has remained their basic political concern ever since [62]. Such a view may be controversial, but it is not easily refuted because trade union support for collectivist measures has invariably stopped short of sanctioning interference with free collective bargaining.

4 Industrial Peace and Industrial Unrest

THE opening years of the new century were ones of industrial peace. The years 1899–1907 were in fact the quietest in the whole period from 1891 (when adequate strike statistics start) to 1933, a year that ushered in another era of industrial calm [19:*326*]. As we have seen, Clegg *et al.* attribute this tranquillity largely to the development of collective bargaining procedures in the well-organised trades. For these authors in fact, 'the development of collective bargaining was the outstanding feature' of the period 1889–1910 [19:*471*].

The form which this development took was twofold. In the first place collective bargaining increasingly came to replace unilateral regulation as the method whereby wages and other working conditions were determined, although in some industries the traditional craft controls continued alongside the more recent collective bargaining arrangements – despite the opposition of the employers to their continuance [19:*155*]. Such collective bargaining over *substantive* questions – conditions of employment – was, however, largely conducted at a local or district level within each industry. Secondly, there developed a system of national, industry-wide procedure agreements. These agreements established a procedure whereby disputes which remained unresolved at local or district level had to be referred to a central joint conference of the industry before any resort to strike action could take place. National procedure agreements of this kind were reached in cotton weaving in 1881, in cotton spinning in 1893 (the famous Brooklands agreement), in boots and shoes in 1895, in engineering in 1898, in building in 1904 and in shipbuilding in 1908. An attempt to establish similar arrangements in printing in 1909 ended in failure [19:*438-9*]. Viewing the system as a whole, it may be said that substantive rules were formulated locally, and *procedural* rules – which enabled substantive agreements to be interpreted, enforced and amended – were formulated nationally [57 :*280–1*].

The logical development of the system would have seemed to be industry-wide substantive, as well as procedure, agreements. In the 1890s there had been national agreements in the printing and shipbuilding industries dealing with specific substantive issues such as the regulation of apprenticeships or the introduction of new machinery; and in 1908 the shipbuilding industry went further and began negotiating pay adjustments on a national basis. In cotton weaving also, pay adjustments were dealt with at industry level and the coal industry had moved a considerable way in this direction since the formation of the Miners' Federation. These, however, were the exceptions, and Clegg has argued that, before 1914, 'it was difficult to discern a definite trend towards industry-wide pay settlements' [20 :*203*].

Phelps Brown has suggested that the system developed in this fashion because wages and other conditions differed so widely from one district to another that it would scarcely have been practicable or useful to deal with these matters in a single national conference, whereas 'rules of conduct were general and could be dealt with nationally'. Furthermore, there were certain rules of conduct which were of crucial significance to employers and which they were anxious to ensure were observed. Phelps Brown refers to the case of the engineering industry :

> The dispute of 1897–8 in engineering had really been about the prerogatives of management – for example, was the decision which man should work on a certain machine one for management alone, or had the union the right to a say in it? The principles agreed to govern such questions were industry-wide in their application, because an employers' federation had sprung up to make the dispute industry-wide [57 :*281*].

To the extent that national procedure agreements were seen by employers primarily as devices for establishing and enforcing their right to introduce new machinery and methods of working, it is clear that little scope existed for the development of industry-wide collective bargaining. In practice, however, not all

42

employers' organisations took so restricted a view of national agreements.

In the period up to 1907 it appeared that, judged by the criterion of industrial peace, collective bargaining worked. After that date, however, strike activity increased, and the whole period down to 1926 – with the exception of some of the war years, when an industrial truce was in operation – was one of unprecedented industrial conflict. Although various writers have seen revolutionary implications in this situation of intense strike activity, it will perhaps be useful to explore first of all the more mundane explanations.

There were, to begin with, a number of defects in the collective bargaining system that had been established. As has been noticed, national procedure agreements could operate in a restrictive fashion. To the extent that they did, one result was to build up discontent among workers at the level of the firm; and since there were no formal institutions capable of resolving conflict at this level – industrial relations being 'generally regarded as external to the firm' [20:*156*] – such discontent found an outlet in unofficial activity. Historians have only too often failed to notice such activity in the years before 1914. The workers' agent at the level of the firm was the shop steward, and Pelling has stated that 'shop stewards had only rarely existed before the war' [54:*151*]. As Clegg has pointed out, however, this is simply not true [20:*37*]. In engineering, particularly, the introduction of new machinery and payments by results raised numerous issues on the shop floor, and increasingly workers elected shop stewards to represent them in dealings on these matters. 'By 1909 stewards were being elected . . . in most of the major centres, and their number and functions continued to grow'[19:*432*]. Cole commented many years ago on the tendency for these prewar engineering shop stewards to form Workshop Committees for the purpose of bargaining with management over piece rates [22]. In the Amalgamated Society of Engineers a serious rift appeared between the national leadership and local militants, and of course during the war the situation became very much more difficult. But engineering was not the only industry where central disputes procedures increasingly failed to resolve local issues. In cotton the procedures failed to deal quickly enough with disputes which arose over 'bad material', so that the unions became increasingly hostile to the agreements in the period up to 1910. In shipbuilding, disputes over craft rules remained endemic.

But the major problem confronting the collective bargaining system was the need for wage adjustments. In 1908, a depression year, there were major stoppages in cotton, shipbuilding and engineering, all arising from a refusal to accept wage reductions. In earlier years, as we have seen, unions and employers had sometimes sought to avoid clashes over wages by means of sliding-scale agreements, but these had become increasingly unpopular with workers, who 'wanted the growing power of their unions to secure a steady wage for them, and an end to the cuts of the bad years' [19:472]. Resistance to wage cuts became all the stronger in the early years of the twentieth century because of the rising cost of living. The cost of living had been falling in the last quarter of the nineteenth century, and because wage rates had held up relatively well, real incomes had risen. After 1900, however, wages fell behind a rising cost of living and real incomes fell. The economic background of rising prices and lagging money wages lay at the root of the difficulties which confronted the collective bargaining system. Union leaders might continue to believe in its advantages, offering as it did a guarantee of union stability, but the rank and file would judge the system by its economic results. It had failed to prevent a steady erosion of their purchasing power, and this circumstance gave an edge to all the various disputes which arose making them harder to resolve than they would otherwise have been. The conflict over wages reached its pre-war climax in 1912, with the national Miners' strike over the demand for a national minimum wage. This was the biggest stoppage the world had yet seen.

A final and obvious defect in the collective bargaining system was its coverage. In 1910 total trade union membership stood at 2,565,000. As a proportion of that part of the occupied population which the unions might reasonably expect to organise, this figure represented 17 per cent [19:466]. Although this proportion was nearly three times as great as in 1888, unionists

44

were still a small minority. Virtually all the well-organised trades, with the notable exception of the railways, had well-established collective bargaining machinery, but since the vast majority were unorganised they were necessarily outside the collective bargaining system. Most workers therefore did not have access to any established procedures which would handle their grievances. If the latter accumulated, sooner or later a major explosion could be expected, and this is what happened after 1910 just as it had happened in the late 1880s. Unorganised workers had suffered from the rise in the cost of living, and in the period of high employment after 1910 they had the chance to do something about it.

Although the conflict in the organised sector of British industry was an important, and perhaps neglected, feature of the period after 1907, the upheaval in the unorganised trades was even more remarkable. It was during the years after 1910 – the period of high employment – that trade unionism at last began to acquire a firmer foothold among the mass of lower-paid, lesser-skilled workers, and it did so in the aftermath of a spontaneous wave of strike activity. The extension of unionism to these groups had been a feature of the upsurge of 1889–91, but most of the gains made by the 'new unions' had wasted away. In 1910, in fact, two of the major general unions reached their lowest point since 1889. As Turner has remarked, the movement of 1889, despite its symbolic impact, achieved only a narrow footing: 'It was not for another twenty years that the "New Unions" launched, in the industrial struggles that immediately preceded the First World War, upon an extension that carried them by 1920 to a rivalry in strength with the long-established craft organisations and cotton operatives' unions, and with the more recently-consolidated miners' associations' [67:*171–2*]. In the unorganised sector conflict developed of its own accord: the unions came in to organise it. As an official of the Engineers remarked in 1913, referring to the role of the Workers' Union in the Black Country strikes: 'The Workers' Union is not so much directing the strikes as following them, and is making members by the thousand' [36:*56*].

In 1913 the number of strikes rose to its peak figure before the

First World War, and the increase in union membership – 719,000 – was the greatest that had yet taken place [55 : *154*]. All the general unions expanded rapidly in this period, for they were ideally adapted to the task of organising the masses of workers in industries, occupations or localities that had been neglected by established unions [34 : *195–6*]. The general union that expanded most rapidly, however, was not of the 1889 vintage : it was the Workers' Union, formed in 1898. The membership of this union was a mere 4500 in 1910, but by the outbreak of war it had reached 143,000, and by 1919 the union had 495,000 members and had become the largest single trade union in the country [36 : *80*]. The exceptional performance of this organisation was partly due to the policy of its leaders who 'showed an unprecedented willingness to invest in growth' [36 : *76*].

The mounting industrial conflict on the eve of the First World War led some historians to suggest that Britian was on the verge of a revolutionary upheaval. Such a suggestion appeared plausible in view of the other disturbing developments that were taking place outside the industrial sphere at this time – the crisis over Irish Home Rule, the violent suffragette campaign and the government's conflict with the House of Lords over the budget. G. Dangerfield felt that all these various developments had something in common. They were part of a general revolt against parliamentary institutions, and they were sounding the death knell of Liberal England [26]. The picture of a Britain saved from revolution only by the outbreak of a world war makes good historical drama, but most writers are inclined to doubt its accuracy. Pelling, for example, has written : 'Our conclusion must be, therefore, that the labour unrest was only coincidental with the acute phases of the Irish and Women's Suffrage questions. It had its own independent and sufficient causes; and in any case, it owed little to feelings of disappointment with parliamentary institutions or existing political parties' [55 : *164*].

The view that the strike movement of 1910–14 was capable of precipitating a revolutionary situation really hinges on two related propositions. The first concerns the influence exerted by 'Syndicalism' in the trade union world, and the second the

46

likelihood of a 'general strike' taking place. Syndicalism was a revolutionary ideology which, originating in France, began to win adherents in this country in the period leading up to the war. Its special relevance to the contemporary situation lay in the fact that it rejected parliamentary institutions and orthodox political activity, and emphasised instead the value of direct industrial action. The idea was that the workers should undermine the capitalist system by strikes and then take over the running of industry themselves through their own organisations. Syndicalism was an ideology which held considerable appeal for militant unionists at a time of rapid expansion of organisation because unlike orthodox socialism it implied no curtailment of union activity by the state. The practice of Syndicalism, however, required the reorganisation of the trade union movement on 'industrial' lines. Hence, one measure of the progress of the new ideology is the degree of reorganisation achieved.

Syndicalists were at their strongest in the South Wales coalfield, yet their scheme to reorganise the South Wales Miners' Federation was decisively rejected at a ballot in 1913 [3:322–7]. On the railways a new industrial union did indeed emerge in 1913 – the National Union of Railwaymen – and syndicalists played some part in this development. An important factor in the formation of the N.U.R. was, however, the experience of joint working gained by the unions during the railway strike of 1911 [4:325]. Whatever the origins of the amalgamation, the syndicalists' triumph was in any case incomplete. The key union of engine-drivers and firemen did not come into the scheme. Syndicalist influence continued into the war and beyond it; its measurable achievements were, however, negligible.

The second proposition concerns the possibility of a general strike on the eve of the First World War. Dangerfield suggested that, but for the war, there would have been a 'general strike' in Britain in 1914 – the 'great General Strike of 1914, forestalled by some bullets at Sarajevo'[26:400]. The prognostication of an imminent general strike arose out of a new development which occurred in April 1914: the informal establishment of the Triple Alliance.

The Alliance linked together the Miners' Federation, the

N.U.R. and the Transport Workers' Federation. Since all these organisations had been involved in large-scale strikes in 1911–12, their joining together seemed to threaten industrial action on a truly massive scale. In the coal and railway industries, there were problems which could have led to stoppages in 1914, and it was therefore possible to argue that, had one or other industry been involved in dispute, the Alliance would have been brought into operation and something like a general strike would have followed. This theory has been effectively demolished by G. A. Phillips : 'In no respect did the launching of the Triple Alliance in 1914 anticipate or entail an imminent "general strike" ' [58 : 66]. There was no certainty of a dispute either in the railway or mining industry, but even if one had occurred there is no evidence whatsoever to suggest that the Alliance could or would have been brought into operation. Events after the war were to show clearly enough the difficulties involved in concerting action between the three industries [5].

The practical difficulties apart, however, it is clear that the intention of the founders of the Alliance was not to maximise industrial conflict, let alone precipitate a revolutionary crisis on syndicalist lines. They had a number of objects in view. In the first place there was a desire to concert action simply because action taken by one of the parties unilaterally inevitably had consequences for the other two. The national coal strike of 1912 cost the major railway union £94,000 – the sum paid in compensation to members laid off as a result of the dispute [5 : 98]. Secondly, the parties saw the Alliance as a means of enhancing their bargaining power. They had the idea that the three industries should arrange to terminate their agreements with the employers at the same time. The *threat* of a combined stoppage would be sufficient, it was felt, to secure the unions' demands in each industry. Viewed in this light, the Alliance was designed to reduce rather than increase conflict, by creating a power which neither the employers nor the state would wish to put to the test. 'The attraction of the alliance . . . lay in the promise of bloodless victories' [58 : 65].

If these were the intentions, they fell far short of achievement. As P. S. Bagwell has pointed out, the constitution of the Alliance

48

made no reference to the simultaneous termination of agreements [5 : *104*], and its wording 'suggests that its framers were more concerned to maintain freedom of action for each union than they were to establish an instrument for the conquest of industrial power' [5 : *102*]. The disastrous post-war record of the Alliance, culminating in Black Friday 1921, bears out this suggestion to the full [5; 13 : *ch*. 7].

5 The First World War

THE First World War did much to develop the pre-war system of collective bargaining. Hitherto employers' organisations had played a major role in developing the system, but the initiative now passed to the state [20:*127*]. In 1915 the government introduced compulsory arbitration as a means of resolving disputes during wartime. We have seen how the weaker unions had long believed that such a system would work to their advantage, and so it now proved. Their ability to achieve results, and therefore attract members, was greatly enhanced. The arbitration system, and government control of certain industries, also encouraged the development of industry-wide pay settlements. National settlements for the railway industry began in 1915, coal followed in 1916, and engineering in 1917. 'By the end of the war the practice of industry-wide pay adjustments had spread to other munitions industries, most sections of transport, and a number of other manufacturing and service industries' [20:*204*].

The centralised handling of pay settlements encouraged the development of industry-wide organisation, both of employers and unions. Trade union federations, such as the Transport Workers' Federation or the newly established National Federation of General Workers, came to exercise a vital role in co-ordinating at national level the bargaining activity of member unions. Both of these federations launched national programmes on behalf of their membership during 1917 and 1918. The Transport Workers secured national pay awards for carters, tram and bus workers, and dockers, while the General Workers obtained national advances for workers in the chemical, aluminium and aircraft industries, gas undertakings, brick-making and flour-milling [13:*80–3*]. Similarly, on the employers' side national awards stimulated industry-wide organisation. Thus federations of employers in gas and chemicals were formed after national awards had been issued in these industries [20 : 128].

These developments arose as expedients to deal with the wartime situation, and compulsory arbitration certainly could not be expected to continue beyond the war period. The report of the Whitley Committee in 1917, however, had important consequences for the post-war system of industrial relations. The Committee recommended that within each industry joint councils representative of employers and unions should be set up – at national, district and works level. The Committee's main concern was to improve the machinery of collective bargaining in the well-organised trades [15 : 104], but the latter were, in general, indifferent or hostile to the scheme. In this situation, the report became chiefly notable for its influence in trades which had been outside the collective bargaining system before 1914. Here, on the initiative of the government, a large number of joint councils were set up at national level. By 1921, seventy-three had been formed, and although some subsequently foundered there were still forty-seven in existence in 1926 [20 : 205]. The establishment of the councils had the effect of perpetuating the industry-wide associations of employers and unions, for these came to constitute the two sides of the new bodies. The councils also perpetuated to a large extent the wartime practice of industry-wide pay adjustments – this practice also continued in some well-organised trades which did not come into the scheme. The Whitley Committee's recommendations thus played a large part in extending industry-wide collective bargaining far beyond its pre-war confines. This was the case not only in the private sector, but also in public employment where, after some early hesitations [36 : 97], the government implemented the scheme in full.

The extension of collective bargaining was a process which of course entailed an extension of the area of trade union recognition. Employer recognition was vital to union growth. This was particularly true in the white collar sector, as G. S. Bain has demonstrated [6], and the war and immediate post-war years constitute a landmark in the evolution of white collar unionism

51

[6 : *ch.* 9]. The influence of recognition as a factor making for union expansion was reinforced during the war and immediately after it by labour market conditions. Employment had been high in the pre-war years 1910–14; it remained so during the war and the short post-war boom that followed. By 1920 labour had experienced a decade of near full employment. These years of high employment and rising prices saw sustained trade union growth. In 1920 total union membership stood at 8,348,000 : a remarkable figure which represented almost 48 per cent of the labour force – even in 1913 only 20 per cent had been organised [6 : *142*].

Although the war years undeniably strengthened the formal institutions of collective bargaining they also, as is well known, brought a major upheaval in certain sectors of industry. The pre-war growth of shop steward activity in the engineering industry has already been noted. The war, however, brought a tremendous increase in the number of problems which had to be handled on the shop floor, and hence the number of stewards rose rapidly. The most critical shop floor problems arose over the 'dilution' schemes introduced by the government in 1915 : schemes which entailed the suspension of craft union controls in the munitions industries and the introduction of semi-skilled and unskilled labour into what had been the province of skilled workers. Dilution and the undermining of craft status brought a wave of unofficial strikes in the major engineering centres from 1915 onwards, and out of this unofficial activity there emerged the famous Shop Stewards' Movement.

It is necessary to distinguish this Movement, which sought to build up a new and revolutionary industrial organisation of the workers based on Workers' Committees of shop stewards, from the general growth in the number and influence of stewards. As J. Hinton has pointed out : 'Shop stewards' organisation within the workshops spread rapidly during the war, but the shop stewards' *movement* . . . became established in only a handful of the largest munitions centres' [33 :*16*]. Ordinary shop steward activity in fact received formal recognition in the engineering industry, for in 1917 and 1919 national agreements were signed between the engineering unions and the Employers' Fed-

52

eration which provided for the recognition of stewards and work-shop committees as bodies of first instance in industrial negotiations [46 : *ch.* 4; 47 : *172–5*].

It is, however, the unofficial movement which has attracted the attention of labour historians. Various writers have dealt with the revolutionary characteristics of the movement [61; 39; 21], but the most recent and thorough study is that by Hinton [33]. He has examined the structure of the engineering industry, and concludes that a necessary precondition for the emergence of a revolutionary Workers' Committee in any centre was technological backwardness. In those centres where technology was 'archaic', notably the Northern areas, the privileges of the craftsmen were still intact when war broke out, and wartime dilution was thus experienced as a major shock, stimulating extreme militancy. In regions, such as the Midlands, where methods of production were more advanced, dilution had already progressed some way before 1914, so that there the craftsman was not presented with a sudden, fundamental challenge to his status [33 : *16*].

Since the attack on craft privileges was the principal factor leading to the emergence of the Workers' Committee movement, that movement rested on somewhat insecure foundations from the beginning. While some of the leaders were anxious to break down craft barriers, accept new machinery and methods, and forge an alliance among the skilled, semi-skilled and unskilled in the industry, it was difficult to carry through this policy when mass support for unofficial activity had been built up on the issue of defence of craft privileges. It was perhaps not surprising that in the end, 'craft conquered class goals among the rank and file of the movement' [33 : *16*]. The truth was indeed that the interests of the craft workers – who formed the backbone of the unofficial movement – and those of the mass of lesser-skilled workers were very far from being identical, and the war years witnessed mounting friction between the craft and the general unions in engineering. As Hyman has pointed out, the changes in workshop practices which so outraged the craftsmen were in many ways advantageous to the lesser skilled [36 : *82–3*], while on the other hand the craftsmen's successes (as, for example, in

53

securing exemption from conscription for military service or in restoring old working practices after the war) greatly aroused the resentment of the lesser skilled. There was much bitterness between the craft and general unions, for the latter – and the Workers' Union in particular – 'gave institutional form to the conflicts of interest which existed within the engineering labour force' [36 : *123*].

The divisions within the engineering labour force do not receive great emphasis in Hinton's study; instead, the focus there is on the clash between the Workers' Committees and the state. The war years are seen as a time of 'domestic repression', and Hinton makes use of Belloc's idea of the 'servile state' to demonstrate how government, big business and trade union officialdom combined to impose an increasingly rigid discipline upon the industrial work force [33 : *ch*. 1]. Belloc's notion that the pre-war social legislation of the Liberal government foreshadowed the coming of a 'servile state', in which workers would be persuaded by the government to exchange freedom for security, has been criticised by Emy [29]; none the less Hinton has argued that there was a continuity between pre-war social reform and wartime labour controls, and that the latter were primarily repressive in intent. 'Confronted by employers, state and trade union officialdom, the shop stewards' movement saw all three forces as collaborating in the construction of the servile state. It is as a revolt against this emergent servile state that the political aspect of the shop stewards' movement is primarily to be understood' [33 :*55*].

Davidson has strongly criticised this view of wartime collectivism as an emergent bureaucratic tyranny [27; 28] : 'Statutory labour regulations were the last and not the first resort of wartime labour administrators in their efforts to cope with a critical shortage of manpower. They were drafted very reluctantly by civil servants, many of whom . . . had always opposed labour regimentation, but who were forced by the munitions crisis to place the military before the social repercussions of wartime controls' [28 :*66*]. In Davidson's view the 'servile state' is a myth. He has further suggested : 'perhaps the key to the failure of the Shop Stewards' Movement lies . . . in the irrelevance of its aims to the experience and aspirations of the mass of British labour' [28 : 67].

The status of the craftsmen may have been threatened, but the mass of semi-skilled and unskilled workers benefited from the wartime economic regime. The national arbitration awards were in the form of flat-rate increases, which meant that the lower paid made the highest relative gains, and traditional differentials were narrowed. Dilution also operated to the advantage of the lesser skilled [48]. The Whitley scheme led to the establishment of collective bargaining machinery in many industries where it had hardly existed at all before. There were to be many disappointments after 1920, but the war and immediate post-war years undeniably enhanced the living standards of the majority of wage-earners.

6 The General Strike of 1926, and the Turning-Point of 1932–3

THE General Strike of 1926 has often been regarded as a major turning-point in the history of trade unionism. Bullock sees it as such [13 : *ch.* 13], and Pelling also treats it as a major landmark [54]. In one important sense it obviously was an important landmark: it was the first and last occasion on which massive industrial action was used in an industrial dispute in Britain.

Beyond this, however, it is hard to pinpoint precisely in what ways the event marked a turning-point. The defeat of the strike certainly did not mark the abandonment of revolutionary goals by the trade union leadership, for these had never seriously been espoused. The whole course of events leading up to the strike, and the manner in which it was called off after having achieved nothing for the miners, provide the clearest possible evidence of trade union reluctance to challenge the power of the state. As Bullock himself has noted: 'although a General Strike was constantly referred to and threatened between 1919 and 1926, no one on the trade union side ever worked out the problems of organisation involved, leave alone prepared for armed insurrection' [13 : *100*]. These were years of substantial development in trade union organisation. They witnessed a series of important union mergers: the formation of the Transport and General Workers' Union, the National Union of General and Municipal Workers, and the Amalgamated Engineering Union. They saw major developments in the organisation of the T.U.C. Yet the able union leaders of the period had left on one side the problems of organising a General Strike. In the end the General Strike threat proved to be pure bluff. As Mason has remarked: 'when the Government refused to give way to threats and chose instead to oppose the strike as a threat to the constitution, the

T.U.C. were cornered. They could either retreat and be humiliated or stand and fight, for which they were totally unprepared' [49 : *14*; 25 : *ch.* 11].

If the defeat of the General Strike did not bring a revolutionary era to an end, perhaps it nevertheless closed an era of industrial militancy. The year 1926 certainly separated a period of industrial conflict from a period of relative peace. During the years 1919–25 an annual average of nearly 28 million working days were lost through strikes and lock-outs. During the period 1927–39 the average was a little over 3 millions [17 :*3*]. These figures might seem to indicate that the General Strike brought about, as Knowles suggested, 'new attitudes, not only to general strikes but to all strikes' [40 :*4*]. In an important article written some years ago Clegg challenged this view and argued that it was 'possible to provide an explanation for industrial peace which pays scant attention o he part played by the General Strike' [17 :*8*]. His argument focused on the incidence of national disputes – official disputes which affected the whole of an industry. In the period up to 1926 the very high number of working days lost was caused by the frequent occurrence of national stoppages [17 :*4*]. After the mid-twenties the number of national disputes declined, hence the drop in working days lost, but they did not end with the General Strike. In 1929, 1930, 1931 and 1932 there were national stoppages in the textile industries. After 1932, however, national disputes disappear entirely from the scene until December 1953.

On this basis, it is the years 1932–3 which constitute the turning-point rather than 1926–7. Hyman, writing more recently, has suggested that the 1930s constitute 'something of a watershed in the history of British strikes' [37 :*26*]. Clegg offered two reasons to explain the frequency of national disputes in the period 1919–25 :

First of all collective bargaining on a national scale, and particularly over national industry-wide changes in wage rates – a rare exception at the beginning of the century – had, as a result of the first world war, become the general practice in British industry. Secondly, rapid fluctuations in the price

57

level, requiring both upward and downward adjustments in the wage rates, made it impossible for these national negotiations to function smoothly [17 :4].

A possible objection to the latter point might seem to lie in the fact that further price falls, and hence wage-reductions, after 1925 did not result in a continuing high level of national disputes. However, as Clegg pointed out, the downward pressure on wages was in general less severe in this period. Thus, even at the height of the depression in 1931, 'reductions reported to the Ministry of Labour did not amount to as much as one-fifteenth of the total reported in 1921' [17 :5]. In those sectors where reductions were severe after 1925 (mainly the export trades) national disputes still occurred – hence the coal crisis of 1926 and the series of disputes in textiles during 1929–32. Given the importance of the twin factors of rapid price fluctuations and national collective bargaining, Clegg's doubts concerning the significance of the General Strike are well justified : 'It remains true that the General Strike came at a turning-point between industrial conflict and industrial peace; but can this be shown to be much more than an accidental coincidence ?' [17 :28]

If there is reason to doubt the part played by the General Strike in bringing to an end a period of severe conflict, it is beyond serious dispute that the strike had no fundamental effect on the level of union membership. In 1920, as we have seen, total membership reached the 8 million mark, but with the onset of depression the following year it went into rapid decline. The decline was almost continuous from 1920 right through until 1933, when total membership stood at 4,392,000. Very slight recoveries occurred in 1924 and 1929, as prices and employment turned briefly upward, but the downward trend was quickly resumed. The 1924 'recovery' was not sustained in 1925, so it does not appear that the General Strike stifled an incipient revival in membership. Of course, some individual unions, particularly those actually involved in the strike, suffered badly in 1926. The Miners are an obvious case, and Hyman has argued that the strike was a critical turning-point in the fortunes of the Workers' Union [36 :135]. The massive decline in the latter organisation's membership, however, came between 1920 and 1923, and signs of recovery thereafter were only slight. It was indeed the years 1920–3 which did the damage, and the collapse was greatest in those organisations – the general unions in particular – which had expanded most rapidly between 1910 and 1920. By 1923 the National Amalgamated Union of Labour had lost 65 per cent of its membership, the Gasworkers' and General Labourers' Union 60 per cent, and the Workers' Union over 70 per cent [36 : *128–9*]. This was a reverse almost on the scale of the early 1890s.

Trade unionism in the 1920s was, however, stronger than appeared from the membership statistics. Despite declining numbers, the area of employer recognition of trade unions was not drastically reduced as it had been in earlier periods. Furthermore, as S. Pollard has observed, there was a sense in which membership loss was 'often more nominal than real', in that no weakening in solidarity occurred [59 : *113*]. In such a situation (which did not, of course, apply in the most recently organised sectors) 'mass blacklegging was simply inconceivable at the workshop level' and 'the authority of the trade union was little impaired even among those who had fallen out of membership or had never been in it'. The massive solidarity displayed by the strikers during the 1926 General Strike provides the best evidence as to the effective strength of British trade unionism.

Turning aside from the question of the General Strike's significance, and examining the period 1920–33 as a whole, it must be said that it was in many respects a barren one so far as the development of trade unionism and industrial relations were concerned. Even the positive achievements – the union mergers and T.U.C. reorganisation – had their origins in the previous period, and in any case the more general attempts to rationalise the structure of the union movement ended in deadlock in 1927 [42 : *99–101*].

Perhaps the single most surprising and remarkable development was the growth in the influence of the T.U.C. [45 : *187–8*]. This development was surprising because it occurred against all the odds. The early schemes to enhance the authority of the T.U.C. General Council, so as to enable it to function as a central federation of trade unions, came to nothing [16:*227–8*]. The General Council's intervention in the mining crisis of 1925–6 ended in disaster. Finally, there was the episode of the Mond–Turner talks in 1928–9 [44; 15: *Pt* 4; 20:*130–3*]. The leadership of the Council, and Bevin and Citrine in particular, had required considerable courage and imagination to enter upon these discussions with the Mond group of employers, since in the aftermath of the General Strike it was only too easy for the Communists and their sympathisers to portray the Council's action as a further 'betrayal' of the workers. Yet the talks, which promised so much in the way of progress in reconstructing industrial relations in Britain, in the end achieved nothing – not because of any lack of creative thinking on the T.U.C. side, but because the majority of employers as organised in the National Confederation of Employers' Organisations preferred to stand still.

Yet despite the failures and false starts, the authority of Congress grew. The basis of that authority is the subject of a study by Allen, who analyses the changes in the organisation of the T.U.C. that occurred during the years 1918–27 [1: *ch.* 13]. He concludes:

> By 1927 the T.U.C. had the making of a trade union bureaucracy akin to the civil service. By comparative standards its scale was small, but it was sufficient to have an impact on the nature and effectiveness of trade union action. Within the limits of trade union traditions and practices, the decisions of the General Council came more and more to be based on information supplied by specialists. . . . From this stage the T.U.C. was able to accumulate authority amongst trade unions which had no constitutional basis but which was derived from its knowledge and integrity. It thereby contributed more positively than ever before to the Trade Union Movement [1:*184*].

It was an ironic circumstance that one of the ways in which the new authority of the T.U.C. was demonstrated was in the clash with the second Labour government in 1931: a clash which played a major part in that government's downfall. Relations between the trade union movement and the first Labour

60

government in 1924 had been somewhat strained [43], and the T.U.C.'s experience during that time had helped it to define its own sphere of action in relation to that of the Labour Party [1 : *180*]. The situation in 1929–31 was, however, rather different. An aspect of the T.U.C.'s development which a number of writers have commented upon was its increasing sophistication in economic affairs and, as a consequence, its capacity to evolve well thought-out policies for dealing with the problems of unemployment and industrial depression [59; 13 : *ch.* 16; 42 : *114–19, 130–1*]. These policies were unorthodox, and challenged the conventional wisdom of the time, but they were realistic. The Labour Party, by contrast, had not evolved a strategy for dealing with economic crisis. As R. Skidelsky has pointed out, its leadership tended to focus on a long-term socialist solution for all the ills of society, but this focus prevented it from devising policies which would deal with the immediate problems of unemployment and depression [65 : *xii*]. As a consequence, it simply fell back on orthodox deflationary policies, and so of course in 1931 came up against the adamant opposition of the T.U.C.

Interestingly enough, a very similar situation developed in Germany at this time, where the unions came into sharp conflict with the Social Democratic Party. The latter refused to accept that there was any middle ground between pure capitalism and pure socialism, and so supported a traditional deflationary policy. The unions on the other hand pressed for an expansionist solution, with easier credit and public works programmes. As E. Kassalow has suggested in relation to the German experience : 'in many respects the sometimes cautious, less doctrinaire tactics of the unions were better adapted to the real social needs and opportunities of the day' [38 : *44–5*]. There was, however, nothing automatic about this. Both the German unions and the British T.U.C. had equipped themselves to make this kind of contribution; the T.U.C. as it had existed in 1920 would have been incapable of giving such a lead. Although the outcome in 1931 was hardly a satisfactory one to the labour movement, the blame did not lie with the General Council, and its prestige was enhanced rather than diminished by the stand which it had taken.

7 Conclusion

TRADE unionism had a chequered history in Britain between 1875 and 1933, but, despite the great fluctuations in membership strength during the period, few historians would quarrel with the proposition that in the twentieth century unionism was stronger and more securely rooted than it had been in the nineteenth. Even in 1933, after thirteen years of decline, membership was still over four times as great as in 1888; and after 1933 a long period of expansion began.

Scholars are divided over the reasons why unionism has expanded over the long run. Many would explain union growth by reference to social stratification. Thus, unionism might be said to have expanded as a result of the emergence of a 'homogeneous working class'; an assumption that is implicit in Pelling's history [54:89–90]. A recent study by Bain, Coates and Ellis has, however, strongly criticised theories which specifically link union growth with class and status [7]. A different approach is one which links union growth with employer recognition and government support: an approach exemplified by Bain's study of the growth of white collar unionism [6].

There is indeed much to be said for viewing trade unions in terms of their relationships with employers and the state. A union's capacity to influence working conditions, and therefore to attract and retain members, is intimately bound up with these relationships. It is the great strength of Clegg *et al.* that their *History* focuses not on unions in isolation but on the process of interaction among unions, employers and government. Above all, it focuses on the evolution of collective bargaining: the principal means by which unions have been able to influence working conditions. It has sometimes been objected that such an approach neglects the political and ideological dimensions of union activity. As Flanders has pointed out, however, in an invaluable essay on trade unions and politics, unions are constrained by their needs as institutions to subordinate political to industrial activity [30:*24–37*]. A union that is to survive and grow must give priority to the short-term economic interests of its members, for this is the common bond that holds organisation together.

Select Bibliography

THE works listed below are those to which reference has been made in this study. The place of publication is London, unless otherwise stated.

[1] V. L. Allen, *The Sociology of Industrial Relations* (1971). A collection of essays, many of which deal with the history of trade unionism in Britain. A large section of the volume is devoted to the history of the T.U.C., and the essay on the reorganisation of 1918–27 is particularly useful.

[2] R. P. Arnot, *The Miners*, vol. 1 (1949). This and subsequent volumes constitute the standard history of the Miners' Federation of Great Britain.

[3] R. P. Arnot, *South Wales Miners* (1967). One of a number of regional studies of mining unionism – of particular importance in view of developments in South Wales in the period.

[4] P. S. Bagwell, *The Railwaymen* (1963). One of the best studies of unionism in an individual industry.

[5] P. S. Bagwell, 'The Triple Industrial Alliance, 1913–22', in Asa Briggs and John Saville (eds), *Essays in Labour History 1886–1923* (1971). The essay discusses the factors which led to the formation of the Alliance, its record, and the reasons for its failure.

[6] G. S. Bain, *The Growth of White-Collar Unionism* (Oxford, 1970). An analysis of the process of union growth among white collar workers in Britain. Bain stresses the importance of three factors: employment concentration, employer recognition and government action to promote recognition.

[7] G. S. Bain, D. Coates and V. Ellis, *Social Stratification and Trade Unionism* (1973). A critical survey of the literature concerned with the interplay of social stratification and trade unionism. An extremely useful book.

[8]   F. Bealey and H. Pelling, *Labour and Politics, 1900–1906* (1958). Contains a discussion of Taff Vale and its political consequences.

[9]   J. D. M. Bell, *Industrial Unionism: A Critical Analysis* (1949). A useful study of union structure, which is strongly critical of the case for 'organisation by industry'.

[10] A. Blum, 'Why Unions Grow', *Labour History*, IX, 1 (Winter 1968). A critical survey of various theories of union growth. Although primarily concerned with the American experience, the article has a more general application.

[11] Asa Briggs, 'Introduction', in Briggs and Saville (eds), *Essays in Labour History 1886–1923* (1971).

[12] R. Brown, *Waterfront Organisation in Hull 1870–1900* (Hull, 1972). As much a study of the local labour movement as of waterfront unionism, but valuable none the less.

[13] A. Bullock, *The Life and Times of Ernest Bevin*, vol 1 (1960). Much more than a biography, this is one of the best studies of the labour movement between the wars.

[14] R. Challinor, *The Lancashire and Cheshire Miners* (Newcastle, 1972). A useful regional study, of particular interest because of the role of the Lancashire Miners in the formation of the Miners' Federation.

[15] R. Charles, *The Development of Industrial Relations in Britain 1911–1939* (1973). Somewhat misleadingly titled, this work deals with some major landmarks in the evolution of collective bargaining – the Industrial Council of 1911, the Whitley scheme, the 1919 Industrial Conference, and the Mond–Turner talks. Contains much useful information and some valuable insights, but the book suffers from the somewhat rigid and cumbersome way in which the author has structured his material.

[16] Lord Citrine, *Men and Work* (1964). An autobiography, covering Citrine's career up to 1939. Contains much of interest.

[17] H. A. Clegg, 'Some Consequences of the General Strike', *Transactions of the Manchester Statistical Society* (January 1954). One of the few serious attempts to assess the significance of the General Strike.

[18] H. A. Clegg, 'The Webbs as Historians of Trade Unionism 1874–1894', *Labour History Society Bulletin*, no. 4 (Spring 1962). Part of a symposium, to which V. L. Allen and A. E. Musson also contributed.

[19] H. A. Clegg, A. Fox and A. F. Thompson, *A History of British Trade Unions since 1889*, vol. 1 (Oxford, 1964). Based to a large extent on original research, this work is indispensable. It does not go beyond 1910, however, and volume 2 has still to appear.

[20] H. A. Clegg, *The System of Industrial Relations in Great Britain* (Oxford, 1970). This is a standard industrial relations textbook, but it places the present system in historical perspective, and reveals some serious gaps in the work of labour historians – most notably their failure to study the history of the work group.

[21] K. Coates and T. Topham, *Industrial Democracy in Great Britain* (1968). A collection of readings dealing with the development of the movement for workers' control. Revised edition issued in paperback in 1970, under the title *Workers' Control*.

[22] G. D. H. Cole, *Workshop Organisation* (Oxford, 1923). Essential reading for those interested in the history of shop stewards and unionism in the workplace.

[23] G. D. H. Cole, 'Some Notes on British Trade Unionism in the Third Quarter of the Nineteenth Century', *International Review for Social History*, II (1937), reprinted in E. M. Carus-Wilson (ed.), *Essays in Economic History*, vol. III (1962).

[24] G. D. H. Cole, *A Short History of the British Working Class Movement* (1948 edn).

[25] W. H. Crook, *The General Strike* (Chapel Hill, N.C., 1931). This is a most valuable study of the General Strike weapon, which centres upon the British experience of 1926. The best study of its kind.

[26] G. Dangerfield, *The Strange Death of Liberal England* (paperback edn, New York, 1961).

[27] R. Davidson, 'War-Time Labour Policy 1914–1916: A Re-Appraisal', *Journal of Scottish Labour History Society*, XIII (1974).

[28] R. Davidson, 'The myth of the "Servile State"', *Labour History Society Bulletin*, no. 29 (Autumn 1974). An essay in review of Hinton's study of The Shop Stewards' Movement [33]. A perceptive and well-informed criticism.

[29] H. V. Emy, *Liberals, Radicals and Social Politics, 1892–1914* (1973).

[30] A. Flanders, 'Trade Unions and Politics', in Flanders,

Management and Unions (1970). An important essay which analyses the nature of trade union political behaviour. A number of other essays in this volume are of interest to the labour historian.

[31] A. Fox, *A History of the National Union of Boot and Shoe Operatives* (Oxford, 1958). One of the best individual union histories.

[32] R. Harrison, 'The War Emergency Workers' National Committee, 1914–1920', in Briggs and Saville (eds), *Essays in Labour History 1886–1923* (1971).

[33] J. Hinton, *The First Shop Stewards' Movement* (1973). The focus of interest in this study is the contribution of the Movement to the development of revolutionary theory.

[34] E. J. Hobsbawm, *Labouring Men* (1964). A most valuable collection of essays on labour history – an indispensable source for the study of 'new unionism'.

[35] E. J. Hobsbawm, 'Trade Union History', *Economic History Review*, 2nd ser., xx, 2 (August 1967). An essay in review of Clegg *et al.* [19], that criticises the basic assumptions upon which the work is based. A good reflection of the ideological divisions amongst labour historians.

[36] R. Hyman, *The Workers' Union* (Oxford, 1971). A most stimulating study of a very important, but much neglected, union.

[37] R. Hyman, *Strikes* (1972). A short study of the nature and development of strike activity in Britain. Aimed more at the sociologist than the historian, but of some value to the latter.

[38] E. M. Kassalow, *Trade Unions and Industrial Relations: An International Comparison* (New York, 1969). A survey of trade unionism and industrial relations in Western Europe and America. A useful introduction to comparative labour history.

[39] W. Kendall, *The Revolutionary Movement in Britain* (1969).

[40] K. G. Knowles, *Strikes: A Study in Industrial Conflict* (Oxford, 1952). The classic study of the subject.

[41] J. Lovell, *Stevedores and Dockers* (1969). A study of waterside unionism in London, 1870–1914.

[42] J. Lovell and B. C. Roberts, *A Short History of the T.U.C.* (1968). A fuller account of the T.U.C. in the period up to 1921 is to be found in B. C. Roberts, *The Trades Union Congress, 1868–1921* (1958).

[43] R. W. Lyman, *First Labour Government, 1924* (1957). A valu-

able study, which includes an account of the government's relations with the unions.

[44] G. W. McDonald and H. F. Gospel, 'The Mond–Turner Talks, 1927–1933: A Study in Industrial Co-operation', *Historical Journal*, XVI, 4 (December 1973). The most complete account of the talks yet published.

[45] H. A. Marquand (ed.), *Organised Labour in Four Continents* (1939). The section on Britain provides a good general history of trade unionism between the wars.

[46] A. Marsh, *Industrial Relations in Engineering* (Oxford, 1965). See also, J. B. Jefferys, *The Story of the Engineers* (1945) – the standard union history.

[47] A. I. Marsh and E. E. Coker, 'Shop Steward Organisation in the Engineering Industry', *British Journal of Industrial Relations*, I, 2 (June 1963).

[48] A. Marwick, 'The Impact of the First World War on British Society', *Journal of Contemporary History*, III (1968).

[49] A. Mason, 'The Government and the General Strike, 1926', *International Review of Social History*, XIV (1969). Mason makes use of the Cabinet and Departmental records which became available in 1967.

[50] A. E. Musson, *British Trade Unions 1800–1875* (1972). An excellent introduction to British trade union history, to which the present volume forms a sequel.

[51] H. Pelling, 'The Knights of Labour in Britain, 1880–1901', *Economic History Review*, 2nd ser., IX (1956).

[52] H. Pelling, *America and the British Left* (1956). An analysis of the ways in which popular ideas about American society influenced the attitudes and behaviour of the British labour movement. An unusual and most stimulating study.

[53] H. Pelling, *The Origins of the Labour Party 1880–1900* (Oxford, 1965 edn). The standard work on the subject.

[54] H. Pelling, *A History of British Trade Unionism* (1963). The best short history.

[55] H. Pelling, *Popular Politics and Society in Late Victorian Britain* (1968). This contains a number of essays dealing with labour history, some of which are extremely controversial in nature. None the less, this is a book no labour history reading list should be without.

[56] S. Perlman, *A Theory of the Labor Movement* (New York, 1928). An important study of the nature of trade union behaviour,

written by an American, but drawing upon the experience of a number of countries, including Britain. Critical of the Webbs and of other labour historians of the socialist school.

[57] E. H. Phelps Brown, *The Growth of British Industrial Relations* (1959). Provides an account of the development of the institutions and procedures of industrial relations up to, and including, the great unrest of 1907–1914. A little dated now, but still useful.

[58] G. A. Phillips, 'The Triple Industrial Alliance in 1914', *Economic History Review*, 2nd ser., xxiv, 1 (February 1971). A well executed assault on the idea that the formation of the Triple Alliance threatened to precipitate a 1914 general strike.

[59] S. Pollard, 'Trade Union reactions to the economic crisis', *Journal of Contemporary History*, iv, 4 (October 1969). Deals with the position of the unions during the inter-war depression.

[60] J. H. Porter, 'Wage Bargaining under Conciliation Agreements, 1860–1914', *Economic History Review*, 2nd ser., xxiii, 3 (December 1970).

[61] B. Pribicevic, *The Shop Stewards' Movement and Workers' Control, 1910–1922* (Oxford, 1959). An analysis of the various ideological ingredients that went to the making of the workers' control movement. Contains an interesting Foreword by G. D. H. Cole.

[62] I. Richter, *Political Purpose in Trade Unions* (1973). An application of Perlman's theory to a study of the political behaviour of British trade unions. A lively, if controversial, work.

[63] J. Saville, 'Trade Unions and Free Labour: the Background to the Taff Vale Decision', in Asa Briggs and J. Saville (eds), *Essays in Labour History* (1960). An analysis of the employers' counter-attack of the 1890s.

[64] S. B. Saul, *The Myth of the Great Depression 1873–1896* (1969).

[65] R. Skidelsky, *Politicians and the Slump* (1967). A study of the second Labour government.

[66] E. L. Taplin, *Liverpool Dockers and Seamen 1870–1890* (Hull, 1974). A local study which adds to our knowledge of the unionism of the 'unskilled' pre-1889.

[67] H. A. Turner, *Trade Union Growth, Structure and Policy* (1962). One of the most important works on British trade unionism. Although primarily a study of the development of the cotton

unions, Turner's analysis is of relevance to unionism in general.

[68] S. and B. Webb, *The History of Trade Unionism* (1920 edn).
[69] S. and B. Webb, *Industrial Democracy* (1920 edn). The two books by the Webbs are of course the great classics of British labour history. Although still of great value and interest they are now seriously dated, and more recent studies have greatly modified the Webbs' work.

Index

73